NEW WAY

Adam's bike
and
Is this your hat?

Hannie Truijens

Illustrated by Annabel Spenceley

Is this your hat?   page 2

Adam's bike   page 10

Nelson

Is this your hat?

Helen found a hat in the road and put it on.
"I don't like it," she said.

She went down the road and met Mrs Green.
"Is this your hat?" said Helen.
"I found it in the road."

"No, dear," said Mrs Green.
"This is my hat."
"Oh yes," said Helen.
"Goodbye, Mrs Green."

She went down the road and met Mr Brown.
"Is this your hat?" said Helen.
"I found it in the road."

"No, dear," said Mr Brown.

"This is my hat."

"Oh yes," said Helen.

"Goodbye, Mr Brown".

She went down the road and met Mr Jones.
"Is this Dobbin's hat?" said Helen.
"I found it in the road."

"No, dear," said Mr Jones.

"This is Dobbin's hat."

"Oh yes," said Helen.

"Goodbye, Mr Jones and Dobbin."

She went down the road and into the field.
"This must be your hat," said Helen.
"Goodbye."

Adam's bike

Adam wanted a bike for his birthday.
"I wish, I wish, I wish I had a bike," he said.

Mum came into his room.
"Happy birthday, Adam," she said.
"Look under the bed."

Adam looked under the bed and found a letter.
"Look in the cupboard," it said.

He looked in the cupboard and found a letter.
"Look in the attic," it said.

He looked in the attic and found a letter.
"Look in the garden," it said.

He looked in the garden and found a letter.
"Look in the shed," it said.
He looked in the shed.

He found his present.
It was a bike.
"Look out," said Adam.
"Here I come.
I wished and wished for a bike.
And now I have one."